29 May 03

Happy Birthday!
Get ready for The big
one next year. Prepare!

Love
Ursula

P9-DTO-208

To:

_____

From:

_____

Date:

_____

*a collection of stories,
quotes, scriptures,
and inspirational thoughts*

a Touch

of love for your birthday

HOWARD
PUBLISHING CO.

A Touch of Love for Your Birthday © 2002 by Howard Publishing Company
All rights reserved. Printed in Mexico

Published by Howard Publishing Co., Inc.,
3117 North 7th Street, West Monroe, LA 71291-2227

Contributors: Angie Kiesling, Chrys Howard, Debbie Webb, Philis Boultinghouse

Special thanks to Susan Duke for permission to use her story "Tarnished Tray."

02 03 04 05 06 07 08 09 10 11   10 9 8 7 6 5 4 3 2

Edited by Philis Boultinghouse
Concept and design by Steve Diggs and Friends, Nashville

ISBN: 1-58229-227-2

No part of this publication may be reproduced in any form without the prior written permission of the publisher except in the case of brief quotations within critical articles and reviews.

Unless otherwise noted, Scripture quotations are taken from the Holy Bible, New International Version, Copyright © 1973, 1978, 1984 International Bible Society. Used by permission of Zondervan Bible Publishers. Scripture quotations marked NLT are taken from the Holy Bible, New Living Translation, copyright © 1996. Used by permission of Tyndale House Publishers, Inc., Wheaton, Illinois 60189. All rights reserved.

Our purpose at Howard Publishing is to:
- *Increase faith* in the hearts of growing Christians
- *Inspire holiness* in the lives of believers
- *Instill hope* in the hearts of struggling people everywhere

Because He's coming again!

A Touch of Love for Your
Birthday

Blessing   page 1

Imagination   page 13

Restoration   page 21

Tapestry   page 31

Home   page 43

Dramatics   page 57

Adventure   page 67

Youthfulness   page 81

Blessing

Imagination

Restoration

Tapestry

Home

Dramatics

Adventure

Youthfulness

CHAPTER 1

Blessing

On this day, however many years ago, God gave a gift to the world. That gift was you. There's no one else quite like you. The way you laugh. The way you smile. That special way your eyes light up. The combination of talents that makes you uniquely you.

Did you ever stop to think that in some way, either big or small, your life touches every person with whom you come in contact? Today, on your birthday, let that human "touch" be a return blessing—a thank-you note to God for the gift of life He gave you. As you bless others, you'll be surprised to find how often good things drop into your own lap. Like someone once said, "You can't outgive God!"

PSALM 103:2, 8

Praise the LORD, O my soul,

and forget not all his benefits....

The LORD is compassionate and

gracious,

slow to anger, abounding in love.

3

Life has no blessing like a

prudent friend.

— *Euripides*

Birthdays Are for Giving

When Marjorie passed her fortieth birthday, she began to realize that birthdays were not always a welcome celebration. But she had come to value them more and more in the last five years. It had been five years since her diagnosis of breast cancer. Five years since she'd had surgery. Five years since she'd begun a frightening year of chemotherapy. Five years since she'd discovered the importance of a perfectly matched wig and the fun of wearing fancy hats. Five years since she had told her children that there might not be another birthday celebration in her future. But the chemo and surgery had done their appointed jobs, and Marjorie thanked God daily that she was still celebrating birthdays. Never again to complain about the aging process, only grateful to be aging at all!

This birthday was to be a very special one. In celebration of five cancer-free years and the fact that she was turning fifty, her husband had offered to send her and her two daughters to a famous spa in

Chapter One: *Blessing*

California. It would afford her every relaxation a woman could imagine. She planned to take full advantage of the exercise program as well as spend a day getting a facial and massage. She imagined herself coming back home with brightly colored toenails and a "California" hairdo. Marjorie felt as if her life were just beginning, and she was ready to jump in with both feet!

The day of the trip arrived, and Marjorie joined her daughters, Stella and Hannah, on the airplane headed for luxury. They were shocked to find that the travel agent had not been alert enough to make sure they were seated together, but they took it in stride, and Marjorie sat alone five rows behind her excited daughters. She decided that the relaxation process would begin on the plane and that she would quietly enjoy a book. After all, one of the lessons she had learned in the last five years was that she rather enjoyed her own company.

After carefully tucking away her purse and fastening her seat belt, Marjorie opened her book to chapter 7, ready to immerse herself in the drama of a good John Grisham novel. *What a great birthday present*, Marjorie thought. *I really do deserve a week of focusing on myself.* No sooner had this thought passed through her mind than a woman about her age stood beside her. "Excuse me," she said. "My seat is the window seat."

"Of course," said Marjorie, unfastening her seat belt and standing in the aisle.

Marjorie didn't mind that someone would be sitting beside her, but now she would have to be friendly, and she preferred just to be quiet.

Marjorie and her new travel companion fastened their seat belts and pretended not to notice each other for about three minutes—but this was not like Marjorie, and she soon introduced herself. She found out that her seatmate's name was Elaine and that she was going to San Diego.

"San Diego," Marjorie said. "I am too. My husband is sending my daughters and me to a spa for my fiftieth birthday." Marjorie conveniently left off her cancer story. She'd been defined by cancer long enough.

"How exciting," Elaine responded, her eyes focused on her hands. "I wish I could say

Chapter One: *Blessing*

my trip had a great surprise at the end. But I'm afraid I've already gotten my surprise, and it wasn't so great."

Sensing despair in her new friend's voice, Marjorie asked if there was anything she could do.

"I don't think so," she replied. "You see, my daughter was just diagnosed with breast cancer, and I'm on my way to help her as she begins her treatment."

Marjorie quietly closed her book, knowing that sometimes birthdays are for giving and not just for getting.

$\mathcal{H}$ave you had a kindness shown?
Pass it on;
'Twas not given for thee alone,
Pass it on;
Let it travel down the years,
Let it wipe another's tears,
Till in Heaven the deed appears—
Pass it on.

—Henry Burton

M ATT H E W   5 : 8

"Blessed are the pure in heart, for they will see God."

Blessing

Imagination

Restoration

Tapestry

Home

Dramatics

Adventure

Youthfulness

CHAPTER 2

Imagination

Birthdays. The more you have, the more likely you are to say "Ho hum" when the big day rolls around. After all, you've been here before—maybe more times than you care to remember. But your birthday is special. It's the only day of the year that you can call your own. Why not give your imagination free rein today? Take the time to indulge in a mini mind-safari. You may be surprised at the places you "go" in the next twenty-four hours!

If you're feeling really adventurous, try whipping up a dream "to do" list. Again, let your imagination go wild. Then make at least one item on your list come true. Try for two or three.

Now to him who is able

to do immeasurably more

than all we ask or imagine,

according to his power that is at work within us,

14

to him be glory in the church and

in Christ Jesus throughout all

generations, for ever and ever! Amen.

Ephesians 3:20–21

What do you imagine
Is the best birthday treat?
Would a chocolate cake with shiny candles
Make your day complete?

Or do you need a clown or two
On a cake that's strawberry red
And friends to come and spend the night
But never go to bed?

Is pin the tail on the donkey
A game you like to play?
Or would you rather bowl or skate
To celebrate your day?

Or does your imagination
Include a beach house and a book
While someone serves you dinner
That you didn't have to cook?

Go ahead, you decide;
Choose what you want to do.
That's what birthdays are all about—
Celebrating you!

Chrys Howard

PSALM 66:5

*"Come and see
what God has done,
how awesome his
works in
man's behalf!"*

Blessing
Imagination
Restoration
Tapestry
Home
Dramatics
Adventure
Youthfulness

CHAPTER 3

Restoration

Birthdays are a great time to recharge your battery. If you work, ask for the day off (some companies grant birthdays as automatic holidays) and squander the time with the relaxation activity of your choice: a day at the beach, reading in a shady park, flopping on the couch, enjoying professional beauty services—the list is only limited by your imagination. Or schedule a tête-à-tête with your spouse, a good friend, or God. (He always keeps appointments.)

God set the divine pattern for rest and relaxation when He created the world then stopped to admire His handiwork and rest on the seventh day. Today is a good day to store up your reserves, enjoy favorite memories, and feed your spirit.

MATTHEW 11:29

Take my yoke upon you and learn from me, for I am gentle and humble in heart, and you will find rest for your souls.

Nothing gives rest but the sincere search for truth.

—Blaise Pascal

The Tarnished Tray

Just as Robin and her son were leaving her in-laws' house, her father-in-law, who had Alzheimer's disease, looked at Robin and said, "Wait, Robin, I have something for you."

He left to get something out of a storage building behind his house. When he returned, his eyes were shining. "Robin, this is for you—for your birthday. I know you'll take good care of it."

Robin's mother-in-law touched her arm and whispered apologetically, "I know your birthday isn't until next month. Harold's just not thinking clearly. You don't have to take that old ugly tray, dear."

"Oh, that's OK. I'll take it and see if I can clean it up," Robin graciously replied.

Robin took the large round tray home but left it on her porch for more than a week before taking it out to her husband's workshop. "I wonder what's under all this corroded black gunk? Do you have anything we can use to clean a spot on this tray and see what it's made of?"

Chapter Three: *Restoration*

Wesley found a tiny bit of tarnish remover and a scrap of cloth and began polishing a small area of the tray. To Robin's delight, the spot revealed that beneath the ugly, greenish-brown tarnished layers was a foundation of shining bright brass. She knew, however, that it would take many patient hours of work to make the tray beautiful.

When the actual day of her birthday arrived, Robin repeated a prayer she'd been praying for some time: that her heart be made more like God's. Today as she prayed, she had a mental picture of the old tarnished tray with its one shiny spot. God revealed to her that like the old tray, cleaning her heart would take a lot of hard work. There was a shiny spot that shone brightly for Him, but Robin saw that there was still a lot of grime and dark places of selfishness and greed in her heart that needed cleaning up.

The tarnished tray has become a work in progress for Robin. Each time she polishes another area, she remembers her birthday and the promise of renewal it brought, and she prays that God will continue the same work in her heart—cleaning and polishing until He can see nothing but a reflection of Himself.

Faith never denies reality

but leaves room

for God to grant

a new reality.

—Jim Cymbala

E X O D U S   3 3 : 1 4

"The LORD replied,

'My Presence

will go with

you, and I will

give you rest.'"

Blessing

Imagination

Restoration

Tapestry

Home

Dramatics

Adventure

Youthfulness

CHAPTER 4

Tapestry

Birthdays are a good time to reflect on your life, take stock of your relationships, inventory your blessings. Those familiar faces you encounter every day—your spouse, your children, your next-door neighbor, the convenience store clerk—are like individual threads in a beautiful and complex tapestry. You may not see how intricately they are stitched into the pattern of your life for years to come, but they are there just the same.

Take a time-out today to think of all the people who have made your life the rich tapestry it is.

You have made known to me the paths of life; you will fill me with joy in your presence.

Acts 2:28

*O*ur happiness depends on the habit of mind we cultivate. So, practice happy thinking every day. Cultivate the merry heart, develop the happiness habit, and life will become a continual feast.

—Norman Vincent Peale

Love is the mortar between the bricks

of experience that builds relationships.

—Nancy Corbett Cole

Threads

Joan stretched like a cat as she climbed out of the car. The long drive back to her childhood home had been a grueling one, but anticipation had made every mile marker trigger another memory. Today, many of those memories would assume flesh and blood as she saw again the faces of her aunts, uncles, cousins, and even siblings who had moved too far away for frequent contact. Emily, her six-year-old daughter, would meet many of those relatives for the first time today. And not only was it a family reunion, it was Joan's birthday.

Joan took Emily by the hand and wound her way to the back of the sprawling homestead that belonged to her Uncle Frank and Aunt Edna. The three-story house, older than anyone there, had housed three generations of Beaumonts. Passing through the arbor gate, she saw the gathering of people out back—some faces were familiar; others had completely changed.

Chapter Four: *Tapestry*

After the usual pleasantries, Joan picked up a Styrofoam plate and got in the food line that reached across the shady backyard. Food was always a good icebreaker. Maybe at the picnic table, conversation would flow more easily with these people, who had once been such vibrant pieces of her family puzzle. Now they seemed almost strangers.

"Emily, why don't you try to meet some of your cousins after lunch," Joan encouraged her daughter, who hovered close to her side. Her self-conscious daughter had always found it difficult to make friends. Emily frequently came home from school in tears, the object of other kids' scorn.

"Mommy, why am I different?" she asked her mother as they said their bedtime prayers. It had become a familiar refrain. Speech therapy was helping, but her stutter still surfaced from time to time. Maybe today, among family, things would be different.

"Well, who can this be?" a voice beside her said. Joan glanced up and saw her mother's second-oldest sister, Jane, gazing at Emily. Aunt Jane had always been the odd one of the family. An unusual thread in the family tapestry. She had heard stories about Aunt Jane since her childhood, but she could count on one hand the number of times she had seen her in person.

THREADS

Aunt Jane had never married. Now she was old—probably dying, some whispered. In her younger days she had traveled to exotic places and written brief letters home about this or that adventure, only to emerge with a different tale in some other exotic place weeks later. She'd show up on relatives' doorsteps on Christmas Eve, then disappear again after the midday meal the next day. "I'm a free spirit," she'd say brightly; "gotta go where the wind takes me." And off she went—leaving disgruntled family members behind.

But at least Aunt Jane cared enough to make the cross-country flight to attend the family reunion. Most likely, it would be her last. Here she was, surrounded by her immediate family, and yet they seemed to have little to say to her. She felt drawn instead to a little girl she'd never met before—a distant grand-niece.

"I- I- I'm Emily," the child said gravely as she stared up at the face bent over her. "How old are you?"

"Emily!" Joan scolded, but Aunt Jane laughed and waved off the childish faux pas.

"Don't get upset with her. She has every right to know how old I am," she said, her eyes crinkling at the corners. To Emily, she added, "Tell you what—after lunch, let me show you something special. If you like it, you can have it when I'm finished. And to answer your question, I'll be seventy-seven on my next birthday."

"Is it pretty?" Emily asked.

"Is what pretty, sweetheart?"

"The surprise," Emily said.

"Oh, yes, it's going to be very pretty indeed."

Mercifully, conversation was lively during lunch, and Joan reconnected with two or three cousins while Aunt Jane talked privately with Emily. After the meal, Aunt Jane asked Joan for permission to take Emily to see the surprise. The two slipped away toward the house.

An hour passed.

"Have you seen my daughter?" Joan asked Uncle Frank as he came lumbering down the front porch steps, the screen door slapping behind him.

"Saw her just a minute ago with Jane in the sitting room," he said in his gruff manner. "Whatever they're doing, they're having an awfully good time at it."

Treading lightly down the hall, Joan peeked into the sitting room Aunt Edna had created for "peace of mind" years ago. There, side by side on the flowered sofa, sat Emily and Aunt Jane.

"Those kids don't mean to hurt you," she overheard Aunt Jane say. "They just don't understand you because you're special. You're different from them, but different can be a very good thing. Imagine what a flower garden would look like if all the flowers were the same."

Emily sat quietly beside her great-aunt, taking in her words and watching her work. Aunt Jane's wrinkled hands flew as she worked a needle in and out of an intricate needlepoint on her lap. When the needlework was finished, the fabric would make a beautiful piece of art, suitable for framing.

"You see how tattered it looks from this side?" Aunt Jane said, turning the cloth over. "If you didn't have all these knots and tangled threads here, the top wouldn't look pretty. But when you finish, everything comes out right. It always does in the end."

Joan smiled. Even unusual threads have their place in the tapestry that becomes a family. Without knowing it, Aunt Jane had given Joan a birthday gift she would never forget.

I **praise** you because I am fearfully and

wonderfully made;

your works are **wonderful,**

I know that full well.

My frame was not hidden from you

when I was made in the secret place.

When I was woven together in the

depths of the earth.

Psalm 139:14–15

Blessing

Imagination

Restoration

Tapestry

Home

Dramatics

Adventure

Youthfulness

CHAPTER 5

Home

In *The Wizard of Oz*, a travel-weary Dorothy repeats a phrase that has become synonymous with the famous film: "There's no place like home. There's no place like home. There's no place like home."

And she was right.

Nothing compares with the serenity of home, that place where you not only hang your hat but rest your head and calm your heart. We all need to cocoon once in a while. Being at home gives our physical bodies and our spirits a chance to stoke up for the next foray into life.

PSALM 23:6

Surely goodness and love will follow me all the days of my life, and I will dwell in the house of the LORD forever.

A house is made of walls and beams;

A home is built with love and dreams.

— Unknown

Found at Last

It was sheer coincidence. Or was it providence? Surely some unseen hand had directed the course of Maura's life these past few months for just such a time as this.

Maura Langley had driven out to the old cemetery on the east side of town to photograph some tombstones for a piece she was doing for the fall issue of *Freedom* magazine. Taking some time off from the local newspaper because of office politics, which she felt stifled her creative abilities, Maura was freelancing for a year and enjoying some freedom of her own. At least, as long as her finances would sustain her.

Maura truly was independent, though not by choice. Her mother and father had been killed in a car accident when she was three years old, leaving her to be reared by an aunt on her mother's side. Her only sibling, a sister, had been delivered by the emergency medical technicians at the scene of the accident and adopted by a hopeful couple

Chapter Five: *Home*

in a nearby town. She and her sister had never met. And in spite of her efforts, Maura had been unsuccessful in tracking down any information about her.

The dusty gravel road wound around to the entrance of the graveyard and ended at the gate where Maura parked her 1998 Honda Civic. Maura knew this cemetery well and parked in her usual spot. She noticed another vehicle parked to the side of the road, tipped sharply to the passenger's side on the steep embankment. Her mind registered a minor irritation at the possibility of an intruder. She rarely saw visitors here. Why today, when she needed to work?

Maura grabbed her camera case, two rolls of film, and a half-empty bottle of water that had accompanied her most of the day. With long, brisk strides, she headed into the heart of the cemetery, stopping to use a large concrete crypt as a table for her setup. Adjusting the wide-angle lens for her first shot, Maura caught a slight movement in the top right-hand corner of the frame. Her eyes darted instinctively to the spot, zooming in on what appeared to be a solitary picnic very near a familiar grave.

Lowering her camera, Maura strained to confirm with naked eyes what she'd seen through the lens. There sat a young woman on a blanket near a grave. Her hand gestures suggested that she was conversing. But she was alone.

Maura snapped a few shots and worked her way across the lawn to observe the young woman at closer range. Sure enough, there in front of her own parents' graves, an attractive, dark-haired woman sat eating sandwiches and talking to the Langleys' tombstones. Maura couldn't help but notice a small cake that seemed to occupy a prominent placement in the center of the blanket. It seemed odd to her that there was a candle in the cake.

"Excuse me," Maura ventured. The young woman gasped with surprise. In her preoccupation with her picnic, she hadn't seen Maura coming. "I apologize for interrupting you," Maura continued, "but I'm curious as to why you would be eating a picnic in a cemetery all alone."

"Oh, I do this every year on this date."

"Really?" Maura mused. "Well, you might find this an interesting coincidence. You've chosen to have your picnic with my parents this year. Tom and Sheila Langley. They died in a car wreck twenty-six years ago, and I'm their daughter, Maura. They are buried right beside where you're sitting."

Chapter Five: *Home*

The young woman involuntarily dropped both her sandwich and her jaw. Coughing and sputtering as the color drained from her cheeks, she struggled to speak. Maura moved toward her with a reassuring gesture, hoping to relieve her apparent embarrassment: "It's OK with me, and I'm sure they appreciate the company."

The young woman rose to her feet, asking breathlessly, "Do you know what today's date is?"

"August 28," Maura replied.

The dark-haired stranger motioned for Maura to come closer as she moved toward the headstone. Her fingers ran across the date of death etched in granite as her eyes watched for Maura's expression. "August 28," Maura read, "the day my parents died."

Tears welled up in the young woman's eyes and poured over onto her delicate cheeks as she continued. "Today is my birthday. That is why I'm here. I have been coming here since I was sixteen to celebrate my birthday with my parents. You see, I was born on the day my mother and father died in a car wreck twenty-six years ago. I never met them, but I'm their daughter Mattie."

Intense emotion gripped Maura's heart as her mind wrestled to adjust to the implications of the facts she'd just been presented. This was her sister—her long-lost sister—whom she'd never met. Instinctively and longingly, they searched each other's faces for recognition. And as if on cue, the two sisters ran into each other's arms and wept in an unforgettable embrace until the torrent of tears had passed. Maura and Mattie Langley had found each other in the only spot on the earth—a burial plot—that tied them together.

"Oh, Maura," Mattie sobbed, "I never knew I had a sister. No one ever told me. I've felt so alone my whole life," she continued. "Year after year, I've come here on the anniversary of our parents' deaths and my birth. It has always been such a sad day for me. But this was to be my last. I had come to say good-bye. You see, I'm getting married next month and will be moving to the West Coast. What if you hadn't been here today? I'd have never known you in this life."

Maura touched her baby sister's face with a tender hand. She felt a familiar ache inside for the absence of memories of growing up together: telling secrets, playing dolls, giggling over boys. But a bittersweet consolation swept over her heart. "Mattie, I've experienced another kind of loneliness all

51

these years. You see, I knew I had a sister, and I have grieved so long over losing you. But now my grief is gone. I have found you at last."

The sun set that August day on two sisters sitting together at a significant grave site, sharing peanut-butter sandwiches, a birthday cake, and the stories of their separate lives. The setting of that summer sun marked the dawning of a future together as a family. Forever changed, their histories now merged into a legacy of love that would last their lifetimes and generations to come.

When one door closes, another door opens, but we so often look so long and so regretfully upon the closed door, that we do not see the ones which open for us.

— Alexander Graham Bell

JOB 8:5–7 NLT

*"But if you pray to God and
seek the favor of the Almighty,
if you are pure and
live with complete integrity,
he will rise up and restore your
happy home. And though you
started with little,
you will end with much."*

Blessing

Imagination

Restoration

Tapestry

Home

Dramatics

Adventure

Youthfulness

CHAPTER 6

Dramatics

Remember when you were a kid and your birthday was the biggest day of the year? Well, maybe it played a reluctant second fiddle to Christmas, but inside, it was the event you secretly waited for. The calendar pages never seemed to turn so slowly as when you approached the final countdown of weeks and days until your birthday.

Birthdays were a time for high drama. Lavish cakes. Streamers and balloons. Party dresses. Pomp and circumstances.

Today, why not turn back the clock and get dramatic again? Have some creative fun with your birthday festivities. Whether you've been hankering for a new hair color or a try at skydiving, now's the time to go all out.

The heavens tell of the glory of God.
The skies display his
marvelous craftsmanship.

Day after day they **continue** to speak;

night after **night** they make

him **known.**

Psalm 19:1–2 NLT

There was never yet an uninteresting life.

Such a thing is an impossibility.

Inside of the dullest exterior

there is a drama, a comedy,

and a tragedy.

— Mark Twain

THE DRAMA QUEEN

I am the drama queen,
Or so I've been told
By friends and family close to me
Who say that I'm too bold.

And, yes, I often dress quite strange.
I say I have a flair
For dressing better than the rest
With flowers in my hair.

Most of the year my antics are few,
I try to keep them quiet,
But on my birthday, I just let loose,
They say that I'm a riot!

After all, it's just one day—
It's my birthday, time to cheer!
And then I'll chill and settle down
Until this time next year!

Chrys Howard

ISAIAH 45:6–7 NLT

" I am the LORD, and there is no other. I am the one who creates the light and makes the darkness. I am the one who sends good times and bad times. I, the LORD, am the one who does these things. "

Blessing

Imagination

Restoration

Tapestry

Home

Dramatics

Adventure

Youthfulness

CHAPTER 7

Adventure

Life is an adventure, whether we sign on for the ride or not. At times it's like a roller coaster, at other times like bumper cars, and—mercifully—some days breeze by like glider swings. However they're spent, our days on this earth pass by in an ever-quickening haze of activity. If we're not careful, we can miss the view from the top. And it's those momentary glimpses of glory that make it all worth the effort.

On your birthday, make every minute count. Don't just seize the day; seize the second. Go out of your way to mark this day with adventure. Reach out and grab the brass ring!

You'll always be glad you did.

P SALM 118:23−24 N L T

This is the LORD'S doing,

and it is marvelous to see.

This is the day the LORD has made.

We will rejoice and be glad in it.

*A*dventure is worthwhile.

— *Amelia Earhart*

The Greatest Gift

Maryanne Scott had seen the commercials that advertise a popular arthritis treatment. "I don't want to climb a mountain," the woman on the commercial says. "I just want to play a game with my grandchildren." But Maryanne did want to climb a mountain. It was the one adventure she had never had the opportunity to pursue, and now that she was almost seventy, she felt time was running out. If she didn't do it this year, she was afraid it would take more than that arthritis medicine to get her to a mountaintop.

Maryanne's love for the mountains began many years earlier when she and her husband took annual family ski trips to Colorado. Sunny Florida was a great place to live—and she wouldn't trade it for anything—but the mountains called her back every winter for at least two weeks of skiing.

Chapter Seven: *Adventure*

Always athletic, Maryanne and her husband, Bill, loved bringing family and friends to the mountains to share their enthusiasm for the winter sport.

But her sweet husband had been gone almost five years now, and Maryanne knew that he was the reason she wanted to climb a mountain. He had often commented that he'd love to visit Colorado in the summer to see what the mountains looked like without the snow. But two of their four grown children lived out of state, and for some reason, they always wanted to come home during the summer! Maryanne and Bill couldn't very well be gone when their children were home.

But now an opportunity to climb a mountain had arrived. Maryanne's granddaughter was going to Colorado with her church youth group. Maryanne was a little apprehensive about asking her granddaughter if she could tag along, but she couldn't help herself. This was her last chance!

Three months before the trip, Maryanne invited her granddaughter Cassie to lunch. "Cassie, please don't think I'm a crazy old fool, but I have something important to ask you," Maryanne said in a very sheepish voice.

"What is it, Mamaw? You can ask me anything. You want to know why kids today pierce their eyebrows?" joked Cassie.

"That's a good question, but not the one I have for you today," Maryanne responded. Then she continued, "I have already asked your youth minister, but now I need to ask you. Would you mind if I went on the mountain climb with your youth group? I've always wanted to climb a mountain, and this could be my last chance. My birthday is during the week of the climb, and I would love to turn seventy on the top of a mountain. Wouldn't that be a great celebration?"

Cassie looked at her grandmother as if she had just asked her if she could go with her on a trip to the moon. Actually, a trip to the moon may have seemed more reasonable. At least on the moon gravity wouldn't be a factor, and her grandmother wouldn't fall flat on her face. The space shuttle would certainly be easier on her mamaw than three days walking up a steep mountain. Cassie had made this mountain climb the year before and knew the dangers and difficulties involved.

But Cassie cleared her head of her doubts and looked straight into her grandmother's eyes. "You bet you can go. I would love to spend a week with you on the mountain," Cassie said as she reached across the table to give her a hug. Cassie had always been close to her grandmother and was truly excited about the added adventure this would bring, but she wasn't so sure how the rest of the teenagers would take it. *I'll cross that bridge later,* she thought. *My grandmother is pretty cool. They'll see.*

The weeks following that conversation were filled with excitement as Maryanne and Cassie worked together to prepare for the trip. They developed a walking program designed to build up Maryanne's stamina and a weightlifting program that would ensure that Maryanne could carry her backpack. Maryanne was determined to carry her share of the load each day of the journey, and since she had always kept herself in good shape, she felt pretty confident in her ability to make it to the top successfully.

The day arrived for nineteen teenagers and six sponsors to board a bus and begin their adventure. Maryanne had already elected not to join the teens for this part of the trip. She knew the bus ride would be long, and she needed to save her energy for better things. *After all, at sixty-nine, surely I'm allowed some compromises,* she had reasoned. So two days earlier she had flown to the nearest Colorado town and was resting comfortably in a hotel room as a very noisy busload of "brave babes," as Maryanne called them, trekked across

America. Maryanne could just imagine them laughing and talking loudly with a set of earphones in every teen's ears. *It would have been fun, but right now a good night's sleep is more important,* she thought as she turned off the lamp in her hotel room. *I'll see the kids soon enough.*

Soon enough did come, and Maryanne was surprised to find that she was slightly nervous as she waited for the bus to arrive. She couldn't help but notice the stares of the young mountain crew when she announced that she would be making the trip with the youth group that would arrive that day. *That's OK,* she thought, *it's my birthday, and I'll do whatever I want to celebrate it! I'll bet some of these young 'uns will climb a mountain when they turn seventy too. They just can't imagine it now!*

The bus did arrive, and things began to move very quickly. After hugs and intro-ductions all around, the preparation began. Each person was issued a back-pack; each four-person team, a tent; and each cooking group, portions of the daily meals. Maryanne's backpack was at least ten pounds heavier than she had anticipated. As she bent down to the ground to see if there was anything she could leave, three big boys from her group volunteered to carry some of her load. Maryanne protested, but the young men insisted, and she soon realized that helping each other was a big part of what this mountain climb was all about.

As it turned out, Maryanne witnessed countless acts of kindness— not just toward herself, but toward all of her fellow adventurers. She witnessed one boy carry a girl's backpack for five hours after she injured her foot on a loose rock. She watched in almost disbelief as two other young men carried this same young woman to the top so she wouldn't be left behind. Maryanne listened as words of encouragement flowed from the mouths of these "babes," encouraging her and others to continue on and make it to the top. She thanked God as she soaked up the words of her travel companions, so much younger than she, who offered up prayers for strength and courage.

On Maryanne's seventieth birthday, she celebrated—as she had planned—on the top of a mountain. The view was breathtaking, just as she had imagined for so many years. She cried as she "talked" to her husband about the journey she had just taken, wanting to share it with him in some small way. Then she praised God for His majesty and thanked Him for the best birthday gift He could have ever given her.

"My great and glorious God, I thank you for the beauty of this day and creation You have given us. As I look across these mountains, I marvel at a sky so blue that I am drenched in its color and a lake that looks as if a master painter weaved the best of his palette in every delicate stroke. I am reminded of the song 'How Great Thou Art' and want to sing it at the top of my voice. But, dearest God, now that I've made this journey, I know that this glorious view is not really the greatest gift I've received on this, my seventieth, birthday. No mountain, sky, or lake could equal the inspiration, encouragement, and support that these nineteen teenagers have given me this week. That's the best birthday gift I could ever ask for. And I know You knew it all along. Thank You for giving more than I could ask or imagine."

One thing I do: Forgetting what is behind and straining toward what is ahead, I press on toward the goal to win the prize for which God has called me heavenward.

Philippians 3:13–14

An adventure is only an inconvenience rightly considered. An inconvenience is only an adventure wrongly considered.

—G. K. Chesterton

Blessing

Imagination

Restoration

Tapestry

Home

Dramatics

Adventure

Youthfulness

CHAPTER 8

Youthfulness

Youth has very little to do with age and much to do with state of mind. Whatever marker your birthday celebrates this year, take a moment to remember some of the symbols of your youth:

- ❀ running barefoot through the prickly grass in your backyard
- ❀ catching lightning bugs in a jar with a friend
- ❀ recording your heart's secrets in your diary and locking it with a tiny key
- ❀ riding a bike for the very first time without training wheels
- ❀ dreaming about what you would be when you grew up

Now, take that same spirit and apply it to some new adventure you've been leery of trying or a secret you've not yet ventured to realize. You really can do it—for youthfulness is a state of mind.

ISAIAH 40:31

Those who hope in the LORD

will renew their strength.

They will soar on wings like eagles;

they will run and not grow weary,

they will walk and not be faint.

One can never creep when

one feels an impulse to soar.

—Helen Keller

84

Something More

"Mom, puh-leeeeze," Lauren groaned, her eyes rolling. The mall would close in ten minutes, and her mother, Beverly, was desperately seeking a new skirt. With time running out, she was forced to try an old trick her sister had taught her. She held the skirt to her front and wrapped it from side to side to see if the seams lined up with the outside of her legs. Then she held it to her backside and did the same. Beverly knew that mirrors and seams never lied.

"We would like to inform all shoppers that the doors will close in fifteen minutes," the voice over the loud speaker said. Lauren was thrilled. She had shopped all her twelve-year-old body could shop. Besides that, Lauren was always a bit embarrassed by her mother's unconventional behavior. Beverly knew her daughter had to put up with a lot from her. Their personalities were direct opposites. Lauren was quiet and laid back, just like her daddy. Beverly, on the other hand, sang along with songs on the car radio with the windows

Chapter Eight: *Youthfulness*

down. She often requested extra chocolate chips in her scoop of chocolate chip mint from puzzled teenagers behind the counter at the local ice cream shop. And worst of all, she drove Lauren to school in her bathrobe. Who would ever know, her mother reasoned. Lauren had made her promise *never* to get out of the car.

But today was Beverly's birthday, and Lauren was trying to be as patient as she could with her mother, who had a few years earlier decided that she wanted to stop growing up. "I don't mind growing older," she would say, "I just don't want to grow up." Celebrating her birthday always included something "goofy," as Lauren put it.

Lauren had decided to try being a little "goofy" herself to help her mom celebrate her thirty-fifth birthday. It wasn't easy for a "non-goofy" kid to be "goofy," but she did have a plan.

Once they got home from the mall, Lauren told her mom to go put on some jeans and a sweatshirt. As Beverly returned from her bedroom, she noticed Lauren putting something in her pocket.

"Follow me," Lauren ordered, and they headed behind their house to a hill that overlooked a canyon. Lauren's head moved back and forth as if she were searching for a buried treasure. Soon she said, "This is the place. Sit right here. It might be a little damp, but we'll be OK."

"OK, this is a great place," Beverly replied and plopped down Indian style next to her daughter. "Now what?"

Fifteen minutes of silence passed while the sun sank lower in the sky. Together, mother and daughter watched as gold fused into pink and, finally, purple. There on the side of a little hill, they shared a sunset. At that moment, Lauren took a bottle out of her pocket and blew bubbles toward the horizon. Beverly watched each bubble emerge as they shimmered and floated against the sky.

"Now make a wish," Lauren said quietly. "Happy birthday, Mom."

Beverly was filled with love for a daughter whose nature would be to put candles on a cake but whose love told her she needed to do something more.

God's gifts put man's best

dreams to shame.

—Elizabeth Barrett
Browning

Put on the new self,

which is being renewed in knowledge

in the image of its Creator.

Colossians 3:10